Testimonies

In *Prosperity With A Purpose,* Brian's ___ ___ *El Shaddai* helped us to step out of the daily grind as a means of earning a living and to trust God to supply through a more entrepreneurial route. Prior to this, my income was largely based on the formula: "hours worked" equals "income received." We knew God had to have another way. As we learned more of God's heart to bless His people, we grew confident in His leading to step out of our comfort zone and into a new business—house building. We definitely have more financial risk, but also have more opportunity to see God's hand of blessing. What can we say? He has been more than faithful! Our income in the first half year in this new endeavor was more than double the previous half year's income. And not only did we experience the God of more than enough, but in our endeavor, we also experienced *Jehovah Jireh*, the God of miracles. The first two houses we built sold the same day, less than a week before Christmas, after only a couple of weeks on the market. God is good!

—Frank Remley, Sherwood Park, Alberta, Canada

When Brian Sauder spoke at our church about prosperity, I already knew how to budget and some biblical principles about money. Still, I constantly needed financial help (for food and car repairs) from my church. After that day, I stopped looking at the checkbook balance. I began instead to look to *El Shaddai*, "the God of more than enough" as my supply. Since then I have testified so many times about the many miracles in my finances that my friends got jealous. Now at their request, I am teaching others what the Bible says about money and our God—*El Shaddai*. And yes, lots of times, as God leads, I too, give all that I have in my purse—and the amount in there is increasing. You can't outgive God.

—Dorothy Carlson, Reading, Pennsylvania, USA

It took me years to really accept the concept that God would want to prosper me and my family. Brian was one of the instruments that the Lord used to change my thinking. He helped me to see that if our focus is clearly on God and His kingdom, then prosperity becomes a great blessing and greatly increases our capacity to bless God's people. I began to realize that while God loves the poor and Jesus had a special heart for them, poverty in itself is not of God but is part of the enemy's curse. I began to see God as a generous Father whose provision is always more than enough. During this time, I started a software consulting business which has done quite well through up-and-down economic times, and it has been a great joy to my wife and myself to be able to give financial blessing to the work of God as a result of the prosperity that He has entrusted to us.

—Peter Hartgerink, Russel, Ontario, Canada

Prosperity
With a Purpose

Brian Sauder

House to House Publications
1924 West Main Street, Ephrata, PA 17522

Prosperity With a Purpose

Brian Sauder

© 2003 by House to House Publications
1924 West Main St., Ephrata, Pennsylvania, 17522, USA
Tele: 717.738.3751
www.dcfi.org/house2house

ISBN: 1-886973-65-2

Printed in the United States of America

Contents

Foreword

I have waited a long time for this book! When I read through this manuscript, I couldn't put it down. Brian writes in such a compelling, refreshing way as he shares his own pilgrimage of learning from scripture that our God is not just *Jehovah-Jireh*, our provider, but also *El Shaddai,* a God who is more than enough!

Although I have served with Brian for over twenty years, I found the revelation I received from reading this book to be astounding. I immediately decided to put what I learned into practice. I started to change the way I was thinking. I knew from the scriptures that God took care of my needs, but somehow the understanding that God wanted me to have "more than enough" was a fresh revelation to me. My God was a God who wanted to bless my family so we could give more into His kingdom.

Within a week of reading the manuscript, I experienced two amazing financial miracles. I was speaking in another state, and a man I had never met walked up to me, shook my hand, and left a hundred dollar bill there. Now maybe this happens to you every day, but it certainly has not happened to me. I couldn't wait to call my wife, LaVerne, and tell her about this miracle. But before I could tell her what happened, she excitedly shared with me that an anonymous person had sent us a hundred dollar bill in the mail that same day as a blessing from God!

Well, what can I say? I cannot promise you one hundred dollar bills in the mail the day after you read this book, but you hold in your hands a book filled with truth that will change your life as you line up your thinking with the Word of God. Get ready to experience the Lord's blessing so you can be a blessing to others.

Thank you Brian, for writing this timely book. *Prosperity With A*

Purpose is a practical book with a healthy biblical perspective on God's desire to bless us so we can use His blessing to advance His kingdom. These biblical truths will revolutionize your life!

Larry Kreider
International Director,
DOVE Christian Fellowship International

Introduction

I surprised myself by writing this book. If you told me six years ago that I would be writing a book about money, I would not have believed it. I had heard people talk about experiencing the financial blessings of God, but somehow it never connected with me. It came across as selfish or self-centered and sometimes even greedy. What I couldn't see before, I now see very clearly. The story in this book is an exciting adventure of biblical discovery on which the Holy Spirit led me over the period of these last few years.

"Prosperity with a purpose" is what I now see from the scriptures. God has asked us to fulfill a mission we call the *Great Commission*. Money is simply a tool that God gives us to complete the job He has assigned to us. It would be against His nature to ask us to do a job and yet frustrate us by not giving us the proper tools we need to complete the job.

I hope God's Word and the Holy Spirit bring change to your life as you read these pages. May the Holy Spirit stir your heart so that you pray the same words He asked me to pray..."Teach me to prosper." As you will see from my sometimes humorous experiences, this is a dangerous prayer to pray. In spite of this, you will find an invitation to pray this very prayer at the end of this book. But first, I invite you to hear my story.

Brian Sauder
DOVE Christian Fellowship International
Ephrata, Pennsylvania 17522

CHAPTER 1

Money is a Tool

Picture this with me for a moment. I have hired a carpenter to come and build an extension to my house. All the blueprints are finalized and the contract has been agreed upon and signed. There is just one condition I add to the agreement right before the carpenter is about to start the job. I demand that he complete the job without using any tools…no hammer, no saw, no power tools.

The carpenter, whose business has been slow anyway, grudgingly agrees to give it a try. But he doesn't even know how to begin the project without using his tools. After a few frustrating hours, the carpenter jumps into his truck, and with mud flying from his spinning tires, leaves the job site in frustration. He is heard muttering something under his breath that is best not repeated in public.

This seems like a silly story. No one with a sound mind would hire a carpenter and not allow him to use tools to get the job done. As foolish as this story might sound, it is exactly how many of us view God's financial provision for the job He requires of us.

We have a mission

God has asked His church to fulfill the Great Commission. Would God ask us to fulfill the Great Commission and not provide the resources that we need to complete the job? I do not believe He would. It is against His nature, as I understand it from the scriptures, to frustrate and tease us by asking us to complete a job and then not give us the tools to accomplish that task. Money is simply a tool the church needs to complete its job description. As we examine the scriptures, we will find good reason to expect the financial provision needed for us to complete the task assigned to us.

Could it be that we have more available to us in the area of financial provision than we have asked for? Listen to Paul's words as he is writing to the Ephesian Christians. "I pray also that the eyes of your heart may be enlightened in order that you may know the hope to which he has called you, the riches of his glorious inheritance in the saints, and his incomparably great power for us who believe."[1] Somehow the Ephesian Christians were missing part of their inheritance. Paul was praying for their eyes to be opened to it.

Is it possible that we, like the Ephesians, have missed part of our inheritance in Christ? Has the progress of our mission been slowed because we haven't asked for the tools we need to complete it? Has the spirit of poverty blinded our eyes and kept us from even asking for the finances needed to do the job?

The spirit of poverty

I came across the following definition of the spirit of poverty in Rick Joyner's book entitled *Overcoming the Spirit of Poverty*. Rick states that "the spirit of poverty is a stronghold established for the purpose of keeping us from walking in the fullness of the victory gained for us at the cross, or the blessings of our inheritance in Christ."[2] The accuracy and truth of this definition resonated inside of me as I read it.

The spirit of poverty is a specific and strategic obstacle from the enemy to keep the church of Jesus Christ from growing and prospering. Is it more spiritual to be poor? I used to think it was. But the Lord has convinced me otherwise. I discovered that it does not take much faith to be poor and in lack. It practically seems to happen automatically. In fact, I started to wonder, "Is it really selfish and lazy of us to settle for just barely enough finances to meet our needs?" especially when we have the capacity and ability to raise our faith and believe for much more in order to see the kingdom of God advance.

The rice story

Janet, my wife, and I have always supported missions as a regular part of our budget. This has been our life-style since the first year of marriage. Even before we were married, as singles we supported missionaries because we had a desire to see the gospel go to all the world.

Over the years, we have endeavored to find ways to increase our giving, and a few years ago I had a "grand idea" of how we could accomplish it. My brainstorm was for our family to eat rice and beans for a whole month and give the balance of the money we would save on groceries to missionaries. We had visited South America a number of times on mission trips and enjoyed eating rice and beans as the main food staple while there. I thought it would be a great project for us to do as a family and would model a giving life-style for our children. It seemed like a profoundly spiritual idea to me.

When I shared this deeply spiritual idea with my wife, she gave me an incredulous look and replied, "You can eat rice and beans for a month, but I am not, and I am not going to try and get our children to do it." Quickly realizing that my great idea was not meeting my wife's approval, I remember piously thinking how unspiritual she was and giving up on the idea. As I look back on this embarrassing incident, I would probably have made a good Pharisee that day.

It only hit me a couple of years later how much the spirit of poverty had affected my thinking. I literally wanted to take food away from my wife and children so that we could give a few extra dollars to missions. Just what was wrong with this idea? I discovered this to be a form of poverty thinking. Let me explain why.

I was not believing that God could supply more for us so that we could give more. In my thinking, we were limited to my paycheck. I looked at the income we had and saw that as a ceiling rather than believing God for more money. So I wanted to take food from my children's mouths and give it to missions. What picture of God the Father does that give to my children? It shows them He is a stingy Father, who gives us just enough or barely enough to survive. As we will explore in this book, this is not a biblically accurate picture of God. I realized it was not right for me to show my children this tainted portrayal of God.

Thank God for my wife who could see this was not an appropriate course of action. Although it seemed so spiritual at the time, I should have been raising my faith to believe for more—lots more surplus—not just a few dollars to give to missions. The truth is, I don't want to give $5 more a month to missions. I want to give $50 more a month or $500 more a month!

The icy chill of offerings

Many times whenever the topic of money or finances comes up in church settings, there seems to be an icy chill that spreads across the group. I wondered about this, because every time an offering was taken, I always felt like quickly exiting the building. Why did I feel this way? What was this uncomfortable feeling? Where did it come from? Was it from God or the devil?

This icy chill was not from God convicting hearts to give. I recognize it now as a spirit of poverty sent from hell to strip the church of one of the tools it needs—money. If we closely examine the Bible, we find it communicates about natural riches as well as spiritual riches. What good is it to possess all the spiritual riches in the world if we do not have the means and the natural riches to get them to the people who need them?

Changing our thinking by examining the truth

Would you agree with me that many of the saints of God have to change their thinking in the area of finances? But, how will our thinking change? It will be adjusted by comparing our thoughts to the truth of the Word of God. We need to renew our minds to what the scriptures inform us about finances. Money is a wonderful tool that God wants to give us to accomplish the mission He has given us.

Listen to what John the apostle, a close associate of Jesus, wrote to his fellow believer Gauis, "Beloved, I pray that in all respects you may prosper and be in good health, just as your soul prospers."[3] John's "all respects" included financial prosperity because the context of the letter was advising Gauis about properly helping and taking care of traveling ministers.

Just as the apostle Paul was praying for the Ephesian believers, John, another of the early apostles, is praying here for all things to go well just as the soul of the believer is getting along well. The term *soul* has to do with the mind and will. It is the thinking part of us. Could the way we think and believe actually affect the results we see in our lives?

Let's consider what Darrow Miller, in his book *Discipling Nations*, talks about concerning patterns of thinking that define the existence of peoples around the world.

> So why are people poor and hungry? Except for catastrophic events such as war, drought, or flood, physical poverty doesn't "just happen." It is the logical result of the way people look at themselves and the world, the stories they tell to make sense of their world. Physical poverty is rooted in a mindset of poverty, a set of ideas held corporately that produce certain behaviors. These behaviors can be institutionalized into the laws and structures of society. The consequences of these laws and be-

haviors is poverty. In the West, we used to call it pauper-ism. While the word has been abandoned as old fash-ioned, the concept, poverty of mind, endures. Those with a poverty mind see the world through the glasses of pov-erty. They say or their actions say for them, "I am poor. I will always be poor, and there is nothing I can do about it...." [4]

Does a spirit of poverty cause us to have poverty thoughts that lock us into a life-style of lack? If so, we should resist it with every fiber of our beings!

Teach my people to prosper

In the fall of 1997, I had a vision while worshiping the Lord. I saw a field of corn like I have seen many times in the early part of the summer in Pennsylvania. The corn stalks were young, about eighteen inches high with very healthy, lush green stalks in neat rows with no weeds. The soil was dark and moist but not muddy. It was full of lumps like it had just been freshly tilled. As I watched the field, I noticed there was a slight rustling among the corn stalks; the leaves were gently shaking because a light, refreshing rain was falling on this fertile field.

Then, I heard the Lord repeatedly speak to me, "Teach my people to prosper, teach my people to prosper, teach my people to prosper, teach my people to prosper." I realized that I was being commis-sioned by the Lord to teach a biblically based message of prosperity with a purpose.

This book is part of my response to that commissioning. My dream is to help identify and eradicate the spirit of poverty from the church. The church must be set free to prosper.

I assure you, we will closely examine the scriptures in the follow-ing chapters, but for now ponder these introductory ideas and meditate on them. Could there be something we have been missing? Could the spirit of poverty be wrapped around and strangling you like it once held me? *God, help us to identify if the spirit of poverty has affected our lives!*

NOTES

1   Ephesians 1:18-19
2   *Overcoming the Spirit of Poverty,* Rick Joyner, (Charlotte, NC: MorningStar Publications, 1996), p. 4.
3   3 John 2 (NAS)
4   *Discipling Nations,* Darrow L. Miller, (Seattle, WA: YWAM Publishing, 1998), p.67.

Small Group Study Questions

1. List five specific ways money can be used as a tool to help the church fulfill the Great Commission.

2. What are some symptoms to help us recognize the spirit of poverty in the church? In our personal lives?

3. How can poverty thoughts be related to the spirit of poverty affecting our lives?

4. How can the spirit of poverty affect the way we respond to offerings and other opportunities to give?

5. Reread Darrow Miller's quote on page 15-16 and ask yourself how you might be able to identify with his thoughts.

Prosperity With a Purpose

CHAPTER 2

The Fear of Materialism

Many of us have viewed the Star Wars trilogy of movies. When the movies were originally made in the early 1970's, George Lucas, their creator, made them with the best technology available. I have been told, however, that even though the movies were an overwhelming success, the technology was not available to create them exactly like Lucas had desired and pictured them in his imagination.

As movie making technology improved over the years, it finally developed to the point that Lucas was able to remake all three movies and produce them like he had imagined all along. The movies were then re-released to an anxiously awaiting public. They were a marvelous success.

It seems as though a similar re-creating is happening within the church. Years ago there was a teaching that emerged about prosperity. At the core of this teaching was a revelation of God that was biblical and accurate; however, as the teaching was circulated throughout various venues and parts of the church, it became distorted and taken to extremes. This caused the whole prosperity message to become tainted and subsequently ignored by many parts of the body of Christ.

This is not the first time in church history a truth was taken to an extreme as it was restored to the church. C. Peter Wagner discusses this in his book *Churchquake!*

> Going to extremes while reemphasizing a half-forgotten
> Christian truth is not unusual. Early Calvinists went to ex-

tremes with the sovereignty of God, arguing for double predestination, which threatened to develop into Christian dualism. Early faith healers went to extremes such as choosing not to take medicine or go to a doctor. Early holiness advocates went to extremes and taught complete eradication theology. In all these streams, later generations invariably gravitated a more moderate and more biblical position. When all is said and done, we are now grateful for more emphasis than there used to be on God's sovereignty, on praying for the sick and on personal holiness.[1]

In discovering prosperity with a purpose, we are looking for that moderate and biblical position described by C. Peter Wagner.

Today, there is a prophetic re-releasing of the biblical prosperity message to the church community. This book is a part of the new releasing. There are many scriptures that speak prophetically of a great increase of wealth into the kingdom of God in the last days.

The fear of materialism

Materialism is attempting to meet emotional or spiritual needs with material things. This is a hopeless pursuit. Material things will never satisfy the hunger of the soul. As mentioned in the last chapter, money or material things are simply tools that the Father has given to us to accomplish our mission. Money must be viewed and used as a tool for His purposes vs. a tool for accumulating stuff.

For years much of the church has been living in the fear of materialism—that is, a fear that if God blesses us financially, it will somehow ruin us and cause us to fall away from Him. The classic example that is mentioned from the Bible is Solomon. His enormous wealth (among other things) did seem to cause him to trust less in God. However, to look only at Solomon ignores the many great men of the Bible who experienced abundance and continued steadfast in their love for the Father. There is a long list: Abraham, Isaac, Jacob, Joseph, Noah, Job, Daniel, Jesus and Paul, to name a few. It might surprise you that I included Jesus and Paul in this list. I will elaborate on this in a later chapter.

Job maintained godly character when he was wealthy, when he was destitute and when his wealth was restored again. Job was the same person no matter what his financial state. He maintained his integrity and refused to deny God. See Job 27:5-6.

If we believe the Lord is strong enough to keep us from lust, gossip and other sins that we are tempted with in our Christian lives, why is it that we are unable to believe He is strong enough to keep us from materialism? Is materialism too big or too difficult for Him to handle? Of course not!

Giving defeats materialism

Giving has the power to break the back of materialism. As long as we teach, exhort and practice giving, the nasty hands of materialism will never be able to grasp us in its clutches. I cannot emphasize this enough. As we hold money openhandedly and maintain a practice of liberal giving, we have an insurance policy against materialism and the love of money. If we try to hold on to money, it will ensnare us; but if we hold it loosely, money will never control us. We will control it! *Having money* will never bring joy, but *giving money* can bring great joy.

The scriptures teach in 1 Timothy 6:10 that the love of money is the root of all kinds of evil. The "love of money" is a term that refers to materialism. Please note, this scripture does not say money is the root of all kinds of evil. If this were true, many of the Bible heroes would have been disqualified because they had abundant financial resources.

Verse 17 of this same chapter in Timothy explains further; "Command those who are rich in this present world not to be arrogant nor put their hope in wealth, which is so uncertain, but to put their hope in God, who richly provides us with everything for our enjoyment." Found in this Bible verse is another illuminating definition of materialism: putting our hope in wealth. Instead, our hope must remain in God who gives us abundant provision for our enjoyment and for the completion of our mission. He really loves us that much!

Financial independence

Permit me to introduce another term from Rick Joyner's book that many Christians consider to be a selfish, secular term—financial independence. What if we define "financial independence" as *having the resources on hand that will be needed to obey God's voice*? Too many times we have dismissed or not taken seriously the visions and dreams God has given to us because we have not seen a way for them to be financed. Our excuse for not obeying God is a paltry, "That would be great, but we can't afford it." It is essential to permanently delete the words "we can't afford it" from our vocabulary. These words should be replaced with a positive petition, expecting God's provision, by asking instead, "How is God going to provide?"

Let's look at Noah, one of the Bible characters mentioned previously as an example of biblical persons who experienced abundance and never lost character. When God asked Noah to build the ark, Noah was at a place in his life of sufficient resources to obey. He was financially independent.

There are no scriptures indicating Noah awakened one day and the ark was miraculously finished. There is no record of ravens flying in with pre-cut gopher logs to be fitted into place. The ark was built with manual labor over a period of years. Actually, it seems like Noah did not work on the ark much himself because he was busy preaching. So either his family or hired laborers constructed the ark. It took significant financial resources for Noah to obey God.

Could it be that God wants to provide for us in a similar way? He desires that we have the resources on hand to accomplish His purposes as He reveals them to us.

A similar example from the New Testament is that of Joseph from Arimathea. He was a rich man, a member of the Sanhedrin, who was a disciple of Jesus. Joseph was ready and available when called upon to take Jesus' body and give it an appropriate burial in a rich man's tomb that had never been used before. In Bible times, tombs were used multiple times. His availability and his financial resources played an important role in the death and resurrection of Jesus and the unfolding of the kingdom of God.

If I were honest

To be honest, in the past I actually felt more spiritual or thought it was more spiritual to be in financial lack. I saw it as my cross to bear. In my mind, suffering for the sake of the gospel included not having sufficient or immediate resources. I was shocked to find that this mindset has more to do with a Hindu worldview than a Christian worldview. Listen to what Darrow L. Miller has to say in his book *Discipling Nations*:

> Hindu society actually values ignorance. Imagine you are a development worker who wants to teach poor people in India how to read and write. After all, you reason, illiterate people have little chance of improving their lives. Yet when you get there and begin to grasp the Hindu culture, it slowly dawns on you: In the Hindu system, encouraging the poor to learn is asking them to sin. Hinduism, for its part, has no rationale for why people should be helped. This system asserts that the poor are the poor

because of what they did in their past lives, and their quickest way out of poverty in the next life is to suffer in this one. [2]

The Christian worldview is one of advancing and growing. The Lord does not want me to languish in the same place in any area of my life. He desires to provide the necessary resources to us so there can be growth and increase in every area of our lives.

Are the Jews jealous?

As we look at the scriptures of the New Testament, we understand that one of the anticipated results of the invitation for the Gentiles to come into the kingdom of God was to make the Jews jealous. If we look at the rate of Jews converting to Christ, we have to honestly say it does not appear that they are very jealous. The Jews are not coming to Christ in mass numbers. It is more like a trickle.

Then why do the Jewish people seem to prosper, especially financially? Have they been given special advantages? No, many times the opposite has been true. Has the money been inherited? No, not initially. Have they accepted Jesus as their Messiah? No, in general they have not.

Many Jews today are experiencing financial abundance as a result of the promises given to Abraham generations ago. Simply stated...there is something of *El Shaddai* that is in their family line, whether they are aware of it or not.

In a recent Eagles' Wings ministry email, Robert Stearns stated that he believes the Jewish people's covenant with God still affects generations today:

> Many Jews today believe strongly in their covenant with
> God given to them through Abraham and the promises
> and benefits apply to every area of life including blessing

in finances. These Jews maintain a sense of "holiness" about their business transactions, and indeed all of life, believing all they are doing is blessed and increased by God. This gives a vital sense of purpose and holiness to the pursuit of God's blessing in every area of life, including increase in finances.

Why should Jews be jealous of a church that has not yet learned how to tap into the financial blessings promised to Abraham when they have been experiencing them without Christ? Could this be one of the keys to unlock the end time harvest among the Jews? This just may be one of many reasons God wants His church to experience financial abundance today. As Christians, Jew or Gentile, we have an inheritance in this same family line.

God has unlimited resources, and He will entrust them to us. Will we handle it all perfectly? Probably not, but that is why He wants to teach us. My wife and I give our children an allowance so they can learn how to make wise financial decisions. Will they make mistakes as they are learning? Probably. Are we willing to allow them to make mistakes as they learn? Yes. I believe God is also willing to take a chance on us.

How big is your God-given vision? That is how much He wants to provide. He wants us to complete the visions and dreams He has placed in our hearts, and it is going to take financial resources to do it. First, though, we have to understand that He is the God of "more than enough."

NOTES

[1]   *Churchquake!,* C. Peter Wagner, (Ventura, CA: Regal Books, 1999).
[2]   *Discipling Nations,* Darrow L. Miller, (Seattle, WA: YWAM Publishing, 1998), p.68.

Small Group Study Questions

1. Define materialism.

2. How is materialism defeated?

3. Discuss the difference between you having possessions and possessions having you.

4. How did financial independence affect Noah's ability to obey God?

5. What is a major difference between a Hindu worldview and a Christian worldview?

6. Write some dreams you have had that you dismissed because you thought it would be impossible to afford them.

7. What phrases do you need to eliminate from your speech which confess a financial lack? (e.g., "I'll never be able to afford that.")

CHAPTER 3

Meet El Shaddai

Are you ready to study the Bible? Let's take a look at the scriptures to see what biblical prosperity is all about.

As we read the Bible, it seems there is a progressive revelation of the nature and attributes of God in the Old Testament. Each time God reveals a new attribute of Himself to the children of Israel, a name is given to describe it. For example, in Exodus 15:22-26 after God miraculously intervenes and heals the people, He is called *The God who heals you* or the Hebrew term *Jehovah Rophe*.

It is hard for man's finite mind to understand an infinite being like God. God is so awesome that He can only be understood by considering one of His attributes at a time. Hence, we find this progressive unfolding of God's character in the Bible. In Exodus 17:15, God is revealed as *The Lord is my banner* or the Hebrew term *Jehovah Nissi* after He gives victory to the children of Israel in battle.

One of the first revelations of God found in the Bible is in Genesis 15:2. God is revealed with the name *Adonai* or *Lord*. This is a foundational principle of the Bible. He is Lord of everything. Nothing in the Bible, including financial prosperity, works without the Lordship of Christ. It is a bedrock foundation for every Christian. We will see this principle re-enforced many times as we explore the scriptures to learn about walking in His abundant blessings.

Prosperity with a purpose

Another one of the early revelations of God came with the Hebrew name *El Shaddai*. Abraham was the one who was first introduced to *El Shaddai*. Before we see how God introduced himself to Abraham as *El Shaddai,* let's examine Abraham's first revelation of God. It is found in Genesis 12:1-3.

> The Lord had said to Abram, "Leave your country, your people and your father's household and go to the land I will show you. I will make you into a great nation and I will bless you; I will make your name great, and you will be a blessing. I will bless those who bless you, and whoever curses you I will curse; and all peoples on earth will be blessed through you."

Here in Abraham's original promise of God's blessing is found what I have come to call *prosperity with a purpose.* This verse clearly states that God will bless Abraham, and Abraham will be a blessing to others. This is still what He is saying to us today, "I will bless you and make you a blessing."

This general declaration of blessing becomes a whole lot more specific in Genesis 17:1-6 when God introduces himself to Abraham as *El Shaddai*.

> When Abram was ninety-nine years old, the Lord appeared to him and said, "I am God Almighty; walk before me and be blameless. I will confirm my covenant between me and you and will greatly increase your numbers." Abram fell facedown, and God said to him, "As for me, this is my covenant with you: You will be the father of many nations. No longer will you be called Abram; your name will be Abraham, for I have made you a father of many nations. I will make you very fruitful; I will make nations of you, and kings will come from you. I will establish my covenant as an everlasting covenant between me

and you and your descendants after you for the generations to come, to be your God and the God of your descendants after you."

This term, "God Almighty" in verse one is the English translation of the term *El Shaddai*. Wherever we find the term "God Almighty," it is speaking of the revelation of God using the Hebrew name *El Shaddai*.

The God of more than enough

Who is *El Shaddai*? There are many definitions, and I will give you more than one to paint a broad picture. *El Shaddai*, means the "breasty one." It is sometimes translated the "many breasted one," speaking of more nourishment than ever would be needed. *El Shaddai* is the one who pours out sustenance and blessing. He is all sufficient and all bountiful.[1] And last, my favorite definition and the one we will use...*El Shaddai* is the God of "more than enough."

If we examine this term closely, we find the original blessing God gave to Abraham. He was blessed to be a blessing. Abraham's God would be a God of "more than enough" to him and the generations that would follow. "Enough" is *that which is required to meet our needs*. "More than enough" is *having extra left over to meet the needs of others*.

The God of more than enough changed Abraham's name from Abram, which means, "honored one" to Abraham, which means "father of many." The revelation of *El Shaddai* brought with it a name change and a pronouncement of fruitfulness and posterity.

We read later in Genesis of God's promise coming to pass for Abraham, especially as his servant Laban reports of his great wealth.

Abraham was now old and well advanced in years, and the Lord had blessed him in every way....So he [Laban] said, "I am Abraham's servant. The Lord has blessed my master abundantly, and he has become wealthy. He has given him sheep and cattle, silver and gold, menservants and maidservants, and camels and donkeys. My master's wife Sarah has borne him a son in her old age, and he has given him everything he owns" (Genesis 24:1, 34-36).

We find that not only was Abraham blessed, but he also passed the revelation of *El Shaddai* on to his children. God is the God of Abraham, Isaac and Jacob. In Genesis 25:21, we find Isaac praying for his barren wife Rebekah to get pregnant.

Isaac prayed to the Lord on behalf of his wife, because she was barren. The Lord answered his prayer, and his wife Rebekah became pregnant.

We have no indication why Rebekah was barren, but Isaac knew his father had told him about a God who promised fruitfulness and blessing. His wife's barrenness did not seem to fit the picture his father had painted, so he prayed, and the Lord made his wife fruitful. He had a revelation of *El Shaddai*.

Prosperity for all areas of our lives

When speaking of prosperity in this book, I am using it within the context of finances, but this is only to help us get a handle on God's desire to prosper us. In reality, God wants to prosper us and make us fruitful in every area of our lives. He wants to prosper us in our physical bodies, our relationships, our marriages, our families, our vocations and even our emotions.

Later in Genesis, we read of Isaac prospering in Canaan in a season of drought.

Now there was a famine in the land—besides the earlier famine of Abraham's time…Isaac planted crops in that land and the same year reaped a hundredfold, because the Lord blessed him. The man became rich, and his wealth continued to grow until he became very wealthy. He had so many flocks and herds and servants that the Philistines envied him (Genesis 26:1,12-13).

Isaac personally introduced his son Jacob to *El Shaddai* in Genesis 28:1-3. Let's read it.

So Isaac called for Jacob and blessed him and commanded him: "Do not marry a Canaanite woman. Go at once to Paddan Aram, to the house of your mother's father Bethuel. Take a wife for yourself there, from among the daughters of Laban, your mother's brother. May God Almighty bless you and make you fruitful and increase your numbers until you become a community of peoples."

Here we see *El Shaddai* specifically mentioned in the same breath with "fruitfulness and increase" as Isaac seeks to pass on this revelation of God to his son. I am not sure why; perhaps Jacob did not quite understand what his father was saying, but he ended up getting a personal introduction to *El Shaddai*, complete with a name change just like his grandfather in Genesis 35:9-12.

After Jacob returned from Paddan Aram, God appeared to him again and blessed him. God said to him, "Your name is Jacob, but you will no longer be called Jacob; your name will be Israel." So he named him Israel. And God said to him, "I am God Almighty; be fruitful and increase in number. A nation and a community of nations will come from you, and kings will come from your body. The land I gave to Abraham and Isaac I also give to you, and I will give this land to your descendants after you."

A prosperous soul

Joseph, one of Jacob's sons, was next in line to get the revelation of God Almighty (*El Shaddai*). The God of Abraham, Isaac and Jacob was passed on to the next generation in Genesis 48:3-4.

Jacob said to Joseph, "God Almighty appeared to me at Luz in the land of Canaan, and there he blessed me and said to me, 'I am going to make you fruitful and will increase your numbers. I will make you a community of peoples, and I will give this land as an everlasting possession to your descendants after you.'"

Joseph received the revelation. We find that Joseph had this sense of prosperity in his soul. He had it inside of him. Wherever he was, whatever the situation, no matter how bad, he prospered. He seemed to rise to the top in whatever situation he found himself.

When he was sold into slavery, he prospered there. When he was in Potipher's household, he flourished. Even in prison, he thrived. As the one in charge of the Egyptian government's food supply program, he prospered there. He was the steward of more than enough to help others in their time of need during the seven years of famine. Prosperity was in his heart. He knew God wanted to bless him and prosper him no matter what his present circumstances looked like.

This is what we are looking for…prosperity flowing out of our hearts irregardless of where we are and our current situation. If we have prosperity of heart, we will find a way to prosper, no matter what our circumstances or the opposition facing us. It will not matter the condition of our local economy or if we have a savings account or if we are a single parent, because our prosperous heart will cause us to prosper.

Sometimes when I teach on prosperity, people will misunderstand and say, "Oh, I'll have to get a second job to become more prosperous." This is not it. God might have a better job for you, but it does not mean working twice or three times as hard. God wants to change our thinking about what to expect from Him as we receive a revelation of Him as the God of more than enough. Remember the apostle John's words to Gauis, "as your soul prospers, you will prosper." If we perceive this truth in our hearts, nothing can stop it from flowing out.

Now, please take out your remote control and push *pause*. Hold this thought while we go back and examine another revelation of God as *Jehovah Jireh*.

NOTES

[1] Definition of *El Shaddai* from *Names of God* by Nathan Stone, (Chicago, IL: Moody Press), p.34.

Small Group Study Questions

1. Why do you think God used different names to describe Himself to the children of Israel?

2. Give two examples of how God has met your needs in the past.

3. Why does El Shaddai want to do more than just meet your needs?

4. Abraham passed the blessing of God on to his family line. In the modern world, how can we see this happen?

5. What does it mean to have a prosperous soul?

CHAPTER FOUR

What About Jehovah Jireh?

If you have been around Christians for any length of time, you have probably heard someone at a point of financial need in his or her life boldly declare, "My God shall supply all my needs according to His riches in glory."[1] As you will soon find out, I have prayed this prayer many times for myself. Or, perhaps you have even sung a song with words referring to *Jehovah Jireh*, my provider.

The phrase "My God shall supply all my needs" is a direct quote from Paul writing to the Christians in Philippi. The idea was originally introduced in an Old Testament story of Abraham and his son Isaac where God is called *Jehovah Jireh*. The term *Jehovah Jireh* is another one of the Hebrew names for God describing an aspect of His nature and character. It is found in Genesis, chapter 22. *Jehovah Jireh* when translated to English means, "The Lord will provide."

> Abraham looked up and there in a thicket he saw a ram caught by its horns. He went over and took the ram and sacrificed it as a burnt offering instead of his son. So Abraham called that place The Lord Will Provide. And to this day it is said, "On the mountain of the Lord it will be provided" (Genesis 22:13-14).

If we read the whole story, we find that Abraham was told to offer his son as a sacrifice to the Lord. In obedience, Abraham took his son along to the place of sacrifice. But at the last moment, it was revealed that this was only a test and Abraham's son Isaac should not be offered as a sacrifice. I am sure everyone breathed a collective sigh of relief, especially Isaac. This was good news; however, if Isaac was not the sacrifice, what was to be offered?

God met the need

The offering was provided in the form of a ram caught in a thicket. This miraculous situation was used as an opportunity to introduce the children of Israel (and us) to an aspect of God's nature. He is the God who makes provision for all of our needs.

This is the precise revelation I had of God in the area of finances for most of my Christian life. I believed, prayed and expected this many times—that God would provide all of my needs. I never considered I could ask for more, and to be honest, I felt more spiritual for not asking. If we defined *El Shaddai* as the "God of more than enough," *Jehovah Jireh* must then be the "God of enough."

Do you know what I discovered? God met our every need all of those years when we believed for His provision only. The problem was, there was never anything left over! We had our needs met, but just barely, with 32 cents remaining at the end of the month!

He is more than the God of enough

As I started to ponder the things I am discussing in this book, this revelation of *El Shaddai* would not go away. I felt stirred in my heart to change the focus of my faith and expectation from *Jehovah Jireh* to *El Shaddai*. So I did. I prayed and asked the Lord for more than enough. The most amazing thing began to happen. Literally within months our personal finances began to change. We began to have surpluses. We started to experience more than just having our needs met.

After a year I could not keep it to myself. I felt guilty for not telling people about what I had found in the scriptures and was experiencing in my personal life. I had to reveal God's truth and revelation of His provision to others. It was too good to keep to myself and my family.

To be very clear, the only thing we changed was our faith and expectation of how God was going to supply. I did not get an extra job. No one took an offering for us. We changed what we were expecting and what we were praying (and saying), and our finances began to change.

It eventually dawned on me that the more we live with an understanding of *El Shaddai,* the less we would need the revelation of *Jehovah Jireh.* I say this in the fear of the Lord, knowing that there will always be times when I will need *Jehovah Jireh* to provide supernatural deliverance for me. I certainly do not want to devalue the name of *Jehovah Jireh* in what I am teaching here, but I definitely changed my pattern of thinking and my expectation of what God wants to do in the area of finances. When I started to grasp the concept of *more than enough,* I found it everywhere I looked!

What do I do with the surplus

All of my life I had been thinking in terms of just getting what I needed. For example, in the area where we live it is common to cover the flower beds around the houses with bark mulch to keep the weeds from growing. When I purchased bark mulch to put on the flower beds at our house, I would carefully measure out how many square feet of beds we had and figure how deep it should be covered and then order just the right amount. My intention was to purchase just enough. I didn't want any extra, because I was afraid it would go to waste. I almost always did not have enough to complete the task and had to make another trip to get more.

When I began to understand that my God was a God of more than enough, I started to order more mulch than I needed, asking God what He wanted me to do with the extra. Hmm...maybe my neighbor needs some?

Needs and joys

On a recent trip to Israel, I found this principle alive in Jewish culture. Every Friday night the Sabbath celebration in a practicing Jewish home contains the giving of thanks to God for the bread and the wine after the meal. This practice is not what Christians know as the Lord's Supper. But by giving thanks for the bread, they are expressing appreciation for their basic needs of life being met. By giving thanks for the wine, they are expressing appreciation for the joys of life—the joys are the blessings of God that go beyond the meeting of their basic needs. Jews understand this very important concept about the nature of God.

I have come to understand there are at least two levels of believing and applying faith for provision in the kingdom of God. One level is "my God shall supply all of my needs." The second level is "my God is a God of more than enough." In this second level, God is providing more than enough so not only am I able to meet all of my and my family's needs, but I am also able to reach out and meet the needs of my neighbor or a missionary whom I am supporting. Or maybe I can meet the needs at the local teen center reaching out to the youth of our community. Yes it is prosperity, but it is prosperity with a purpose. Biblically, I believe it is God's will for us to be prosperous and be involved in seeing the kingdom of God expand and fill the earth.

More than enough Bibles

Around the same time I was discovering this revelation of *El Shaddai*, I had just ordered a new Bible. I received the Bible, but it was not the correct size I had ordered. When I contacted the publisher, they instructed me to just send in the first page inside the cover and they would send another. As it turned out, the publisher sent two new ones by mistake. Now I had three study Bibles. All of a sudden I had more than enough Bibles. It seemed like the Holy Spirit was underlining this fresh revelation of God as the provider of more than enough. By the way, I did send the one Bible back to the publisher, but I gave the other to my wife. God blessed me and I was able to be a blessing to Janet.

More than enough for my family

Here is another practical example of how God challenged us to believe for more than enough. Janet and I have always had a dream to have a large family. We desired to have five children. However, every time we shared our desire with anyone, the response was always the same, even from some family and friends. How will you be able to afford so many children? How will you pay for them? We did not really have a good answer at the time, usually halfheartedly responding about God supplying somehow.

In our search for a good answer to this question, we latched onto something we heard from an incredibly godly couple that had a large family. We heard them talking about this same concern and how they handled it. Their kids were all adults now and all serving the Lord so it seemed like a good example to follow.

What they shared was that it took all their time and money to raise their family. In other words, when they had two children, it took all their time and money, and when they had six children it took all their time and money to take care of them. This seemed like a great approach to us, since we didn't know how we were going to afford having five children. So, we latched onto this idea and used it as a point of faith for us as our family grew. We started to tell people that it would take all we had financially to raise our family. It even sounded rather spiritual, saying that we would put all that we had into our children. Sometimes, we even continued by saying that we wouldn't have natural riches, but that our children would be our riches. And as I previously described, that is exactly what was happening until the revelation of God as *El Shaddai*, the God of more that enough.

As God was teaching us this new revelation of Himself, one day my wife came to me and said we needed to stop believing and saying that it would take all we had financially to raise our family. We began to realize that this was believing and expecting God to meet our needs, but not believing that He would meet above and beyond our needs. Our faith and our words had to change if we wanted to see financial abundance. We specifically started to believe and say we would have all of our family's financial needs met and that there would be finances left over for our family to support missionaries, give to others in need or to minister to those in our community.

God showed us we needed to change what we believed, what we said and what we expected. We now have five children and are currently experiencing more than enough time and money for our family. Together, we praise God because He is more than enough!

I have repeated these words "more than enough" so often my children have learned them and looked for places that God was giving more than enough. We started to identify and expect this principle of more than enough in many areas of our family life. I have more examples in the following chapters. Just wait until you hear the story of the one hundred dollar bills!

A divine life-style

God's heart for abundant provision and blessing is at the core of the kingdom of God and its expansion. It is not an idea a preacher came up with in order to take a big offering! This is a scriptural teaching of provision. It is a divine life-style available to all believers.

I do realize there are different seasons including dry times and droughts, and we will examine these more thoroughly later. But, as we will see in the chapters to come, the scriptural pattern is one of more than enough. If we have faith to only meet our needs, then it is likely we will only have 32 cents left after we pay the monthly bills. It is important that we have faith for more than enough. If we have the faith and expectation of God's provision being more than enough, then we will receive more than enough.

I know that many Christians live their lives simply expecting God to only meet their needs. If this is you, I want to challenge you that there is more, much more.

NOTES
[1] Philippians 4:19

Small Group Study Questions

1. What was the occasion for the introduction of the name Jehovah Jireh?

2. How can we change our expectation of God's provision from enough to more than enough?

3. When believing God for more than enough, there is often a surplus. What are ideas that you may have for the surplus?

4. In the Jewish Sabbath celebration, what does the bread represent? What does the wine represent?

5. Why does it matter what we say about our finances? (See Appendix.)

CHAPTER 5

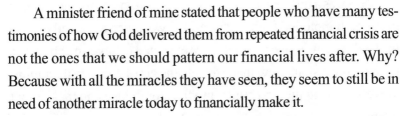

The Contrast

A minister friend of mine stated that people who have many testimonies of how God delivered them from repeated financial crisis are not the ones that we should pattern our financial lives after. Why? Because with all the miracles they have seen, they seem to still be in need of another miracle today to financially make it.

In other words, although they have faith for financial miracles, they have not found faith to receive from God for long term abundant provision. They are still living (wandering) in the desert instead of entering into the Promised Land.

You see, when the children of Israel were wandering in the wilderness, they received a daily miracle for their food called *manna*. It was fresh and new every day. It was miraculous provision.

However, it could not be kept for the next day because any surplus would spoil. There was a complete dependency on God for provision every day. In my perception, this seems to be similar to living by a revelation of *Jehovah Jireh*.

Into the promised land

This was not God's long-term plan for provision. When God took them into the Promised Land, the daily manna stopped. It was no longer an option. In the Promised Land, the children of Israel were expected to live by the principle of sowing and reaping and seedtime and harvest. Let's look at the scripture where the transition happened. It is found in Joshua:

The day after the Passover, that very day, they ate some of the produce of the land: unleavened bread and roasted grain. The manna stopped the day after they ate this food from the land; there was no longer any manna for the Israelites, but that year they ate of the produce of Canaan (Joshua 5:11-12).

This was a different revelation of God's provision for the children of Israel. It included faith, but now they were also expected to farm the land, to sow and reap. They were expected to have an abundance because provisions were made to help the non-Israelis in their midst as well as bring the first fruits into the storehouse and make other offerings.

There was also a whole group of people, the Levites, who were to be supported out of the abundance of the general population. In the desert, their sandals didn't wear out for 40 years, but in the Promised Land their sandals wore out and they had the resources for new sandals. This seems to be similar to living by the revelation of *El Shaddai* that was first introduced to Abraham.

Here is a good biblical definition of the Promised Land as it pertained to the Israelites. The Promised Land was a fertile concept indicating Israel's possession of a place with God in the earth where there was security from all external threats and internal calamity. It is a place of rest, where the people of God can grow and prosper.

If this was true for the children of Israel, then can we boldly ask ourselves:

"What is God's will for Christians in the area of financial provision today?"

"Is it God's will for Christians to live in the desert?"

"Or, is it God's will for Christians to live in the Promised Land?"

God's blessing versus God's miracles

Let's contrast how different living would be in the desert versus living in the Promised Land. Some of us might remember the old television game show called *Let's Make a Deal*. The contestants on the show had the choice of picking cash or prizes from behind two or three doors. The suspenseful part that drew people to watch the show was the fact that the contestants did not know what was behind any of the doors.

If we had the choice of picking between two doors, door number one labeled "God's blessings" and the other door labeled "God's miracles," which one would we pick? A lot of Christians would pick *miracles* because they are fun to watch, but let's consider living in God's *blessings* instead.

I believe the more we live in God's blessings, the less we will have to live by God's miracles. For example, the more we live in God's promise of divine health, the less we will need God's miracles of healing.

Many churches teach that God will heal your body when you get sick. But how many teach divine health, believing that God will give you a divinely healthy life, free from sickness and disease? The more we walk in divine health, the less we will need physical healing.

Let's apply this same thought to the financial realm. The more we live in God's promise of divine prosperity, the less we will need God to do financial miracles in our lives. God's miracles rescue us in times of crisis; however, we can say that living in God's blessings keep crisis from coming.

Comparing God's blessings with His miracles

Blessings	Miracles
El-Shaddai	Jehovah-Jireh
More than enough	God provides our needs
Sowing and reaping in the Promised Land	Daily manna in the desert
Divine health	Miracles of healing
Divine prosperity	Miracles of provision
Keeps crisis from coming	Deliverance in crisis
God works with you	God works for you
Works within natural laws	Overcomes the natural laws
Good car that starts	Miracle needed to start car each day!
Your surplus becomes another's miracle	Need met and no extra left over
Blessings have seed contained in it to plant	No seed to plant

When God intervenes and solves a crisis by a miracle, it is as if He is working *for* us. When God brings blessing into our lives in response to us obeying His Word or sowing seed, it is like He is working *with* us. Miracles are God overcoming the natural laws of the earth. Blessings are God working with the natural laws of the earth, like sowing and reaping, to bring His blessings into our lives. Both blessings and miracles are supernatural and come from God.

Living in God's blessings could bring you a new car that will start every time you need it to start. Living by God's miracles could leave you with a car that requires prayer for a miracle every time you need it to start. I can hear the groaning—too many of us have been there! The amazing thing is that God in His mercy will in some miraculous way help you get your car started. But unfortunately, you will still need another miracle to get it started the next time.

God's nature is seedtime and harvest

Miracles are usually just enough to get us through a crisis, but because God's blessings contain more than enough, the surplus can many times become someone else's miracle, meeting his or her needs. God's blessings are usually the fruit of something we have planted somewhere along the way. Fruits generally have the seeds in them to plant for the next crop. God's miracles are usually once and done. There is no seed in them. God's nature is seedtime and harvest; miracles are God's mercy. Both are supernatural provision and come from God!

Does it take more faith to believe for daily miracles or for a life-style of blessing, healing and prosperity? I think it takes more faith to live a life-style of blessing. God has provided miracles even when there was no faith. Do you remember the water from a rock and manna in the morning? These were miracles God did just to get the children of Israel to stop complaining. There was no great faith there! Could it require greater faith to live a life-style of blessing? The answer from my life experience is "yes."

Please keep in mind as I contrast *El Shaddai* and *Jehovah Jireh*, I am not talking about two separate gods. I am talking about two separate revelations of God's nature given to humanity with finite minds, to somehow gain an understanding of an infinite Being. I am not creating new theology. I am introducing us to a divine aspect of our heavenly Father that some of us have not yet experienced.

Small Group Study Questions

1. What are several reasons for desiring more than just testimonies of God's miraculous provision?

2. How do we know it is God's will for Christians today to live in the Promised Land?

3. Give an example of how life was different for the children of Israel in the Promised Land than in the desert.

4. Having a good car that starts vs. having one that you need to pray for a miracle for it to start each morning is used as an example here. Give another possible modern-day example.

5. Explain in your own words the phrase "God's nature is seedtime and harvest."

CHAPTER 6

El Shaddai Revealed in the Bible

If abundant blessing is really the heart and nature of God, we should find it repeated throughout the Bible. That is precisely what I want to show you in this chapter.

Let's go to Exodus 36:3-7. Please notice the term "more than enough" as it appears in the following scriptures.

> They received from Moses all the offerings the Israelites had brought to carry out the work of constructing the sanctuary. And the people continued to bring freewill offerings morning after morning. So all the skilled craftsmen who were doing all the work on the sanctuary left their work and said to Moses, "The people are bringing **more than enough** for doing the work the Lord commanded to be done." Then Moses gave an order and they sent this word throughout the camp: "No man or woman is to make anything else as an offering for the sanctuary." And so the people were restrained from bringing more, because what they already had was **more than enough** to do all the work.

When is the last time you heard your pastor or any church leader say, "Stop giving…you're giving way too much?" When Moses started a building project, the Israelites were asked to participate by giving offerings. The people gave so much that Moses had to actually issue a decree instructing them to stop. I think most of us would agree the church today has not yet reached this stage.

How about Leviticus?

We have found Bible references to *El Shaddai* in Genesis and Exodus. Now let's look in Leviticus.

> I will look on you with favor and make you fruitful and increase your numbers, and I will keep my covenant with you. You will still be eating last year's harvest when you will have to move it out to make room for the new (Leviticus 26:9-10).

Verse 10 is what we are looking for… "You will still be eating last year's harvest when you will have to move it out to make room for this year's harvest." This sounds like more than enough to me. Last year's harvest was more than enough to meet the needs of the year. The surplus will have to be moved to make room for the new harvest.

Let your thinking be challenged

If your thinking is ruled by thoughts of poverty and lack, some of what I am saying might be hard to swallow. If this doesn't make sense right away, then put it on the back burner, meditate on it and let it cook for a while. See what God shows you. It is a good thing for our thinking to be challenged as we look at the Word of God. We have to allow the Word of God to change us. Listen to what God speaks to Moses and the children of Israel in Deuteronomy. Read these words…

> He will love you and bless you and increase your numbers. He will bless the fruit of your womb, the crops of your land—your grain, new wine and oil—the calves of your herds and the lambs of your flocks in the land that he swore to your forefathers to give you. You will be blessed

more than any other people; none of your men or women will be childless, nor any of your livestock without young (Deuteronomy 7:13-14).

Does this sound like *El Shaddai*? "You will be blessed more than any other people." The key word here is "more." The next chapter states this even more clearly. Let's continue to read in Deuteronomy 8:6-11.

Observe the commands of the Lord your God, walking in his ways and revering him. For the Lord your God is bringing you into a good land—a land with streams and pools of water, with springs flowing in the valleys and hills; a land with wheat and barley, vines and fig trees, pomegranates, olive oil and honey; a land where bread will not be scarce and you will lack nothing; a land where the rocks are iron and you can dig copper out of the hills. When you have eaten and are satisfied, praise the Lord your God for the good land he has given you. Be careful that you do not forget the Lord your God, failing to observe his commands, his laws and his decrees that I am giving you this day.

Here we find similar words describing God's abundant provision. Phrases like "you will lack nothing" and "when you have eaten and are satisfied" simply state this truth in a different way. When you "are satisfied" it means you have more than enough food to satisfy your appetite. It means a smorgasbord, an all-you-can-eat buffet! It signifies you have food left over. This is the pattern that God wishes to establish for us if we will let Him. As God challenges and changes our belief system, our thinking will change. If our thinking changes about finances, our actions will change.

Obedience is essential

Let's pause for a moment to underline something. In the last passage of scripture (Deuteronomy 8), I have included verse six and verse eleven. Both of these verses speak about obedience to God's Word and by implication obedience to His will. The Lordship of Jesus Christ is foundational for what this book is teaching. Lordship is the key to everything in the Bible. No biblical principle, prosperity or otherwise, works properly without the Lordship of Jesus. It is the key to everything in the Bible. He is Lord of the universe, and our wills must always surrender to His. Period!

What is "blessing"?

If we look at Deuteronomy 28, we find both Lordship and prosperity. The first verses speak to fully obeying God (Lordship) and the verses that follow define God's blessings. Let's study this together.

If you fully obey the Lord your God and carefully follow all his commands I give you today, the Lord your God will set you high above all the nations on earth. All these blessings will come upon you and accompany you if you obey the Lord your God: You will be blessed in the city and blessed in the country. The fruit of your womb will be blessed, and the crops of your land and the young of your livestock—the calves of your herds and the lambs of your flocks. Your basket and your kneading trough will be blessed. You will be blessed when you come in and blessed when you go out. The Lord will grant that the enemies who rise up against you will be defeated before you. They will come at you from one direction but flee from you in seven. The Lord will send a blessing on your barns and on everything you put your hand to. The Lord your God will bless you in the land he is giving you. The

Lord will establish you as his holy people, as he promised you on oath, if you keep the commands of the Lord your God and walk in his ways. Then all the peoples on earth will see that you are called by the name of the Lord, and they will fear you. The Lord will grant you abundant prosperity—in the fruit of your womb, the young of your livestock and the crops of your ground—in the land he swore to your forefathers to give you. The Lord will open the heavens, the storehouse of his bounty, to send rain on your land in season and to bless all the work of your hands. You will lend to many nations but will borrow from none. The Lord will make you the head, not the tail. If you pay attention to the commands of the Lord your God that I give you this day and carefully follow them, you will always be at the top, never at the bottom. Do not turn aside from any of the commands I give you today, to the right or to the left, following other gods and serving them (Deuteronomy 28:1-14).

If you obey the Lord, all these blessings will come upon you and accompany you. He will grant you abundant prosperity. The Lord will open the heavens to send rain on your land. If you lend to many and borrow from none, that means you have more money than what you could use for your physical needs. You have surplus to make available to others. God's intention for the children of Israel was blessing, prosperity, freedom and healing. In many ways it is parallel to what we found earlier in 3 John 2. This is blessing. This is God's heart for us.

What is "curse"?

Now that we have defined from the Bible what "blessing" is, let's look at what the Bible says "curse" is. *Curse* is defined in the next few verses in Deuteronomy 28. What we are going to find is that poverty is included in the list of curses.

> However, if you do not obey the Lord your God and do not carefully follow all his commands and decrees I am giving you today, all these curses will come upon you and overtake you.
>
> You will be pledged to be married to a woman, but another will take her and ravish her. You will build a house, but you will not live in it. You will plant a vineyard, but you will not even begin to enjoy its fruit.
>
> You will sow much seed in the field but you will harvest little, because locusts will devour it. You will plant vineyards and cultivate them but you will not drink the wine or gather the grapes, because worms will eat them.
>
> The alien who lives among you will rise above you higher and higher, but you will sink lower and lower. He will lend to you, but you will not lend to him. He will be the head, but you will be the tail.
>
> Because you did not serve the Lord your God joyfully and gladly in the time of prosperity, therefore in hunger and thirst, in nakedness and dire poverty, you will serve the enemies the Lord sends against you. He will put an iron yoke on your neck until he has destroyed you (Deuteronomy 28:15, 30, 38-39, 43-44, 47-48).

We are biblically defining blessings and curses. We find that prosperity is a blessing from God and poverty is a curse from the enemy. We are laying this out as two very clear, distinct, mutually exclusive, separate definitions. This might seem elementary to some, but some Christians get confused about this and start to think that it is more spiritual to be poor and in lack. How can this be when we just read that poverty and lack are the results of disobedience and not obeying the Lord? We must allow the Bible to define these terms for us.

Elisha and the widow

When Elisha helped the widow of one of his prophets with financial provision, he instructed her to gather as many containers as she could find for the oil that was going to be poured out.[1] The oil only stopped flowing when she ran out of containers. Her expectation of God's blessing coincided with how much she received. This is a familiar Bible story, but here again is this principle of more than enough. How much oil did she have? She had more than enough, more than she had containers to fill.

Jehosaphat's plunder

In 2 Chronicles 20, the Lord gave Jehosaphat the victory over Moab and Amman. With his enemies defeated, he advanced to acquire the spoils. When Jehoshaphat and his men attempted to carry off their plunder—a great amount of equipment and clothing and articles of value—it was more than they could carry. In fact, there was so much that it took three days to collect it.

Look for the overflow

In Psalm 23, I read that "I shall not want" and "my cup will be overflowing." If my cup is overflowing it means there is more than enough to fill it. Sometimes I joke with people that they need to be careful if I am pouring a drink for them at a social gathering. I am getting such a revelation of more than enough, I just might keep pouring after it is full and overflow their cup. We find the same thing in Proverbs.

> Honor the Lord with your wealth, with the firstfruits
> of all your crops; then your barns will be filled to over-

flowing, and your vats will brim over with new wine (Proverbs 3:9-10).

Overflowing barns? Remember Joseph who had the overflowing crops for seven years as the minister of agriculture in Egypt? He saved up enough to last for the next seven years of drought. I recall Jesus talking about a guy that had his barns overflowing in the New Testament. In both cases the barns were overflowing, but there was a different use for the surplus on each occasion. What do we do with the surplus? We will discuss this in a later chapter.

Brimming over? This sounds a lot like what we read in Psalm 23 where cups were overflowing. An overflow of new wine sounds like a good thing to me.

Let's finish our Bible study searching for *El Shaddai* in the Old Testament by looking at the book of Malachi.

> "Bring the whole tithe into the storehouse, that there may be food in my house. Test me in this," says the Lord Almighty, "and see if I will not throw open the floodgates of heaven and pour out so much blessing that you will not have room enough for it. I will prevent pests from devouring your crops, and the vines in your fields will not cast their fruit," says the Lord Almighty. "Then all the nations will call you blessed, for yours will be a delightful land," says the Lord Almighty (Malachi 3:10-12).

The Lord promises to pour out so much blessing that we won't have room for it. Here again we find the God-of-more-than-enough!

In this chapter we have examined a lot of scripture. I will give more stories and examples later. However, I want to solidly establish the fact that the scripture teaches God to be a God of *more than enough*. The scripture must be our foundation and our guide.

¹ 2 Kings 4

Small Group Study Questions

1. Can you think of other examples of El Shaddai, the God of more than enough throughout the scripture that are not included in this chapter?

2. How is obedience essential to a biblical understanding of prosperity?

3. Summarize in your own words a biblical definition of "blessing" from Deuteronomy 28.

4. Summarize in your own words a biblical definition of "curse" from Deuteronomy 28.

5. How is "overflow" another expression of more than enough?

Chapter Seven

What About Job?

Some of you may have noticed that as we were looking at the scriptures from the Old Testament regarding prosperity, we did not look at the book of Job. While this is true, it may not be for the reasons you might think. There are many valuable lessons in this book of the Bible. In this chapter we will take a careful look at Job, but let's start first in Matthew chapter six. The lesson here is on worry—worry versus faith.

> Therefore I tell you, do not worry about your life, what you will eat or drink; or about your body, what you will wear. Is not life more important than food, and the body more important than clothes? Look at the birds of the air; they do not sow or reap or store away in barns, and yet your heavenly Father feeds them. Are you not much more valuable than they? Who of you by worrying can add a single hour to his life? (Matthew 6:25-27).

Let's briefly focus on the birds of the air. Do they have enough to eat? If you think about it in the natural, physical sense, you would have to answer, "Yes they do." Generally, birds have more than enough to eat. They have all the seeds, bugs, worms and whatever else they need to be well nourished and survive. The only exception is during seasons of drought when there may be a shortage of food. Let's keep reading.

> And why do you worry about clothes? See how the lilies of the field grow. They do not labor or spin. Yet I tell

you that not even Solomon in all his splendor was dressed like one of these. If that is how God clothes the grass of the field, which is here today and tomorrow is thrown into the fire, will he not much more clothe you, O you of little faith? So do not worry, saying, "What shall we eat?" or "What shall we drink?" or "What shall we wear?" For the pagans run after all these things, and your heavenly Father knows that you need them. But seek first his kingdom and his righteousness, and all these things will be given to you as well. Therefore do not worry about tomorrow, for tomorrow will worry about itself. Each day has enough trouble of its own (Matthew 6:28-34).

Do you think that Solomon had enough of clothes to wear as the king of Israel? In 1 Kings 10:14 it states that King Solomon's income was about 250 tons of gold per year. (You can look it up.) What is the present dollar value of an ounce of gold? It is somewhere around $300 an ounce at the time of this writing. (You can do the math.)

If Solomon measured his income in tons of gold per year, it would appear like the King had more than enough financial capacity to provide more than enough clothing! When Solomon went out to battle, he might not have had his whole wardrobe available but it was only for a short time; he generally had more than enough clothes.

Jesus is talking about physical, natural provision here. He did not use John the Baptist, who only had camel's hair to wear, as His example. He could have, but instead He used Solomon as an example.

Dry seasons

Let's look at the book of Job in context. It is about a season of suffering and dryness in Job's life. The lessons in Job are extremely valuable and the Bible would be incomplete without it. There are dry seasons when God is doing something in our lives to make our roots grow deeper into Him, and we need to discern and persevere our way through these times of drought. Many times pastors and spiritual leaders will help us through these tough, dry times. Just like the birds of the air suffer lack of food during an occasional drought, Christians also experience seasons of lack in their lives. But as we will see from examining Job's experience, the general pattern of God's heart for provision is one of abundance.

In the beginning of the book of Job, it is important to point out that God blessed Job with many financial and material blessings. It was only after the devil came on the scene that God's blessings were interrupted. It was when Job was under the attack of the devil that he was poor, sick and experiencing calamity. This is what the Bible teaches us. Sometimes, Christians get confused about this and think Job is teaching we should be poor and sick. Just the opposite is true. The book of Job is the story of how a man overcame the attack of the devil and what he learned in the process.

The entire book of Job is about a brief season in his life. Although the Bible doesn't specifically say, most Bible scholars believe the whole book covers a time span of between three and eighteen months. In the first few chapters, it talks about the day his cattle and servants were lost. While he was still listening to that report another messenger came in stating his sheep were lost and the shepherds killed. And while he was listening to the sheep report, another messenger came and told him his camels were lost. Finally, while Job was listening to the camel report another messenger came and informed Job that his sons and daughters had been killed. All of this in the same day! And we think we have had some bad days?

His situation grew even worse. The next day, Job himself was physically attacked with sickness. All of this transpired in only two days. I am following Job's losses day by day to underline my point that the time of testing for him was a relatively short period of his life.

The rest of the story

If we look at the end of Job it states that he lived 140 years enjoying the blessings of God in every way. The Bible teaches that Job lived most of his life full of prosperity and God's financial provision. Perhaps this is a new way of looking at this Bible story for you. Actually looking at the scripture will help us to see this point more clearly.

> After Job had prayed for his friends, the Lord made him prosperous again and gave him twice as much as he had before. All his brothers and sisters and everyone who had known him before came and ate with him in his house. They comforted and consoled him over all the trouble the Lord had brought upon him, and each one gave him a piece of silver and a gold ring. The Lord blessed the latter part of Job's life more than the first. He had fourteen thousand sheep, six thousand camels, a thousand yoke of oxen and a thousand donkeys. And he also had seven sons and three daughters. The first daughter he named Jemimah, the second Keziah and the third Keren-Happuch. Nowhere in all the land were there found women as beautiful as Job's daughters, and their father granted them an inheritance along with their brothers. After this, Job lived a hundred and forty years; he saw his children and their children to the fourth generation. And so he died, old and full of years (Job 42:10-17).

Job did not experience 140 years of having boils, poverty, despair and everything going wrong. No, it was a short season of his life in which he learned many valuable lessons. Job's story allows us to learn many theological and doctrinal lessons about the nature and character of God. His actual time of testing was much like the occasional drought that causes the birds of the air to experience insufficient food supplies. The example of Job's perseverance is one we can all honor and duplicate.

Job maintains his integrity

The Bible declares that Job maintained his integrity throughout this time of testing. Earlier I suggested the church might be walking in the fear of materialism. If we are blessed financially, why should we be scared that God's blessing would corrupt or contaminate us? Job is a great example of someone who didn't allow his financial status in life, good or bad, to affect his character and integrity.

Small Group Study Questions

1. For what purposes do you think Jesus used the example of Solomon when teaching about God's provision of clothing?

2. How do we know it was the devil showing up to interrupt Job's blessings? Give chapter and verse.

3. How can observing one season of Job's life cause us to develop the wrong picture of God's overall provision?

4. The Bible states that Job kept his integrity. How does this give us hope that financial blessings will not corrupt us?

5. List some other Bible characters who experienced financial blessings but maintained integrity within their hearts.

Prosperity With a Purpose

CHAPTER 8

Is This Just An Old Testament Thing?

Is this too good to be true? Does God really want to bless us and our families with more than enough money to do all that He has put in our hearts? Sometimes people have difficulty believing that God loves them that much. As I have been teaching what the Bible shows us in the area of financial prosperity, people sometimes ask me if this is just an Old Testament thing. After all, wasn't the revelation of *El Shaddai* an Old Testament revelation to Abraham and the children of Israel?

I can understand the question because almost everything we have looked at so far has been from the Old Testament. I agree…if what I am teaching about the nature of God is valid, it must appear as a theme throughout the whole Bible. These truths do appear numerous times in the New Testament in the ministry of Jesus and Paul. Let us first take a look at a familiar Bible story.

As evening approached, the disciples came to him [Jesus] and said, "This is a remote place, and it's already getting late. Send the crowds away, so they can go to the villages and buy themselves some food."

Jesus replied, "They do not need to go away. You give them something to eat."

"We have here only five loaves of bread and two fish," they answered.

"Bring them here to me," he said. And he directed the people to sit down on the grass. Taking the five loaves and the two fish and looking up to heaven, he gave thanks and broke the loaves. Then he gave them to the disciples, and the disciples gave them to the people. They all ate and were satisfied, and the disciples picked up twelve basketfuls of broken pieces that were left over. The number of those who ate was about five thousand men, besides women and children (Matthew 14:15-22).

In this story of the feeding of the five thousand, it states that they all ate enough food and were satisfied. This is how God wants to feed His people—more than they can eat with extra left over. In this case, it was twelve baskets of food that were left over.

Was there money to feed the five thousand ?

I also find it interesting to examine the disciples' response when Jesus told them, "You give them something to eat," as recorded by Mark in his gospel. Here is Mark's account:

But he answered, "You give them something to eat."
They said to him, "That would take eight months of a man's wages! Are we to go and spend that much on bread and give it to them to eat?" (Mark 6:37).

The disciples did not say the money was not available to them. In fact, none of the gospel records say they could not afford to buy the food. Let's look at Luke's account of the same incident:

He replied, "You give them something to eat."
They answered, "We have only five loaves of bread and two fish—unless we go and buy food for all this crowd" (Luke 9:13).

It seems like they might have had the finances available to them, but were possibly concerned about how to use the money available to them. None of us were there, so we don't know for sure, maybe they would rather have used the money to help the poor. This might be a new way of looking at this Bible story for you, but please consider what these scriptures actually say.

Jesus' ministry

Let us examine another account in Jesus' ministry of *more than enough*. One day as Jesus was teaching from a fishing boat, He wanted to make a practical example for everyone to understand. We find the story told by Luke in his gospel.

> When he had finished speaking, he said to Simon, "Put out into deep water, and let down the nets for a catch."
>
> Simon answered, "Master, we've worked hard all night and haven't caught anything. But because you say so, I will let down the nets." When they had done so, they caught such a large number of fish that their nets began to break. So they signaled their partners in the other boat to come and help them, and they came and filled both boats so full that they began to sink (Luke 5:4-8).

Fishing was the disciples' job. It was how they earned their living. They were not out fishing all night long for a Bible lesson. No, they needed money for their daily provision.

Jesus more than met their financial need. If the fish catch of that day was so big that the nets began to break, and it was so big that it overfilled both boats to the point of sinking, it was definitely more than what they were expecting. Traditionally, most of us have only looked at the later verse where Jesus said the disciples would become fishers of men as the significant spiritual truth taught here. While it is absolutely true that Jesus was teaching this, we cannot overlook the fact that Jesus provided more than enough money for the disciples' paycheck that week. He taught and modeled more than enough.

Is This Just An Old Testament Thing?   67

The parable of the rich man

In an earlier chapter we discussed how we should pray and believe for more than enough finances and then ask God what to do with the surplus. Luke records Jesus sharing a parable of a man that didn't know what to do with the *more than enough* that God had provided for him. Let's read that story.

> And he told them this parable: "The ground of a certain rich man produced a good crop. He thought to himself, 'What shall I do? I have no place to store my crops.'
> "Then he said, 'This is what I'll do. I will tear down my barns and build bigger ones, and there I will store all my grain and my goods. And I'll say to myself, "You have plenty of good things laid up for many years. Take life easy; eat, drink and be merry."'
> "But God said to him, 'You fool! This very night your life will be demanded from you. Then who will get what you have prepared for yourself?' "This is how it will be with anyone who stores up things for himself but is not rich toward God" (Luke 12:16-21).

In this parable Jesus never rebuked the man for having more than enough. In fact he gave no indication that this would not be the normal pattern. He was teaching about what to do with the surplus that God so graciously provides for us. The rich man in the parable moved right out of living the life of faith and giving and moved into self-preservation, materialism and greed. He didn't realize that it was prosperity with a purpose. He did not realize there was a reason for the surplus he was experiencing.

Remember, giving is the very thing that breaks the power of money as an idol in our lives. So, by hoarding it, the rich man actually was empowering money to become a god in his life. He had no knowledge of what to do with the *more than enough.*

We find the same idea underlined in Psalm 49. For those of us with a poverty mindset, our thoughts will automatically apply this scripture to wealthy non-Christians. We don't see ourselves as growing rich, and we would likely be "awed" if it happened. Let's read.

> Do not be overawed when a man grows rich, when the splendor of his house increases; for he will take nothing with him when he dies, his splendor will not descend with him.
>
> A man who has riches without understanding is like the beasts that perish (Psalm 49:16-17, 20).

While this is certainly true for non-Christians, if it is a biblical truth, it should apply to all people, including Christians. We should expect God to bless us financially, but we must understand why He is blessing us. It is for His kingdom. It is to use!

Unlike the rich man in Jesus' parable, King David knew the purpose of his abundance. He was experiencing an abundant level of provision from the Lord, but he knew it was not just for him.

> After David was settled in his palace, he said to Nathan the prophet, "Here I am, living in a palace of cedar, while the ark of the covenant of the Lord is under a tent" (1 Chronicles 17:1).

David knew there was something that wasn't right about this situation. He found that he was provided for, but God's work was not. He saw his personal house was prosperous, but the Lord's house was desolate. He knew inherently in his heart that this was not acceptable. He knew there was a reason for his prosperity.

Paul's ministry

The apostle Paul did not shrink back from teaching on finances either. He wrote the following instructions to the church at Corinth.

So I thought it necessary to urge the brothers to visit you in advance and finish the arrangements for the generous gift you had promised. Then it will be ready as a generous gift, not as one grudgingly given. Remember this: Whoever sows sparingly will also reap sparingly, and whoever sows generously will also reap generously. Each man should give what he has decided in his heart to give, not reluctantly or under compulsion, for God loves a cheerful giver. And God is able to make all grace abound to you, so that in all things at all times, having all that you need, you will abound in every good work. As it is written: "He has scattered abroad his gifts to the poor; his righteousness endures forever." Now he who supplies seed to the sower and bread for food will also supply and increase your store of seed and will enlarge the harvest of your righteousness. You will be made rich in every way so that you can be generous on every occasion, and through us your generosity will result in thanksgiving to God (2 Corinthians 9:5-11).

There is a lot of financial truth for us in this passage of scripture. Let's take a careful look at the content of verse eight, "God is able to make all grace abound to you, so that in all things at all times, having all that you *need*, you will *abound* in every good work." *Having all that you need* sounds like having your needs met and *abounding in every good work* sounds like giving to others after your needs are met. Combining these two thoughts gives us another biblical example of God's desire to bless us with more than enough. To say these scriptures are not referring to money, as some have done, is blatantly taking this passage out of context.

Paul goes on to tell us that God will provide seed to the sower, not to the stingy one who is trying to hold on, hoard and protect what they have. God will add to the one who is generously giving of what they have, lavishly spreading seed in all directions. Proverbs chapter eleven, verse 25 states the man who refreshes others is refreshed himself.

Johnny Appleseed

This brings to mind a traditional American folk hero, Johnny Appleseed. Wherever he went, he sowed apple seeds. We picture him crisscrossing the east coast of the United States in colonial times with a big bag of apple seeds over his shoulder. On his travels, he planted apple trees that would bear fruit.

Wherever we go, we should be sowing finances, e.g., giving to missionaries; giving in special offerings; giving to our children; giving to ministries doing the work of God; giving to the poor; giving to the waitress at the restaurant. Give. Give. Give. To the one who is sowing, more seed will be given! His store of seed will increase.

A friend of mine once told me that his son worked his way through college by being a waiter at a very popular chain restaurant. He told his dad that the staff were reluctant to work on Sundays. "And why would that be?" his dad asked.

"Because all the church people come in and they are notorious for not being generous tippers," was his son's reply. What a sad reflection and testimony this example places upon the church.

Don't eat your seed by spending or storing it all. Plant it. Expect it to grow and bear fruit. No successful farmer would ever eat his seed. He knows he will not have a new crop if he consumes his seed instead of planting it.

Spiritual rubbish

I can recall thinking I was so spiritual when I would tell people that if I had the money I would give it. "Yes, brother, if I had a thousand dollars, I would give it to you for your mission." It sounded so spiritual. It was spiritual...spiritual rubbish! Proverbs 28:19 states, "He who works his land will have an abundant food, but the one who chases fantasies will have his fill of poverty." We can't give what we don't have, so we must quit being spiritually lazy and start believing God for an abundance of finances to give away.

Paul himself never seemed to suffer lack. He always traveled in the most modern form of transportation that was available in his day. It is never recorded in scripture that Paul could not get a boat to the next town because he did not have enough money. The biblical record shows that the Lord directed him to go, and he went. He had the resources that were needed for him to obey God. It was just like Noah, who had the resources he needed to obey God when he was instructed to build the ark.

Acts 24:26 says that the governor Felix sent for Paul frequently and talked with him, hoping that Paul would offer a bribe. Why would the governor Felix, a wealthy man, think that Paul would offer him a bribe? Could it be that Paul had the funds needed for ministry and enough to offer a bribe large enough to impress Felix?

It is for all believers

If you're still not convinced this truth is found throughout the whole Bible, how about a scripture in the New Testament that states the blessings of Abraham are for the believers of the New Covenant.

Christ redeemed us from the curse of the law by becoming a curse for us, for it is written: "Cursed is everyone who is hung on a tree." He redeemed us in order that the blessing given to Abraham might come to the Gentiles through Christ Jesus, so that by faith we might receive the promise of the Spirit (Galatians 3:13-14).

There it is. By faith the blessings given to Abraham are available to both the Jew and the Gentile and also the promise of the Holy Spirit right now as New Testament Christians.

Through Christ, we become heirs of Abraham's blessing. All of the promises of blessing from the Old Testament and the promise of the Holy Spirit are for those who believe, those who are Christians. The Holy Spirit is our teacher. He teaches us to prosper.

We get a total picture of God's heart for us in these scriptures. The church is the seed of Abraham. It is still true today—this is the Father's heart for prosperity and blessings for His children.

At this point you might say, "This is great theory, but how do I apply these truths to my life?" That is where we are going in the next chapter.

Small Group Study Questions

1. Give some New Testament examples of God providing more than enough.

2. What did the rich man do wrong in the parable of the rich man?

3. Give several reasons for developing a life-style of giving?

4. For what reason did Felix bring Paul before him on a regular basis?

5. How do we know the blessing of Abraham is for all believers today?

Prosperity With a Purpose

CHAPTER 9

$100 Bills!

As I was learning the things I am teaching in this book, I felt the Lord was prompting me to pray and ask the Holy Spirit to teach me to prosper. Knowing the scripture reveals that the Holy Spirit is our teacher, I decided to go for it. In prayer one day, I spoke these words, "Holy Spirit, teach me to prosper." I didn't know what I was getting into, but I knew my thinking had to change.

Shortly after praying this prayer, I was in a Sunday morning church service and the speaker was teaching about some deep theological truth from the Bible. In the middle of his message, he stopped and asked this question, "How many people present know how many one hundred dollar bills there are in circulation for every one dollar bill?"

Most of the people were wondering what was going on and why he had departed from his topic. "Are there more one hundred dollar bills in circulation in U.S. currency or one dollar bills?" he repeated again. He paused for a few moments and then went on to give the answer. The answer was that there are 60 one hundred dollar bills in circulation for every one-dollar bill. The speaker said perhaps Christians think in the wrong terms. Maybe we are thinking in terms of one dollar bills when we should be thinking in terms of hundred dollar bills. He then returned to his subject and finished his teaching.

My thinking was challenged

Most of the people in the congregation that day were wondering why the speaker couldn't stay on his topic, but not me. I had a clear sense that the speaker's digression from his sermon was specifically for me. Within two weeks, I was attending a leadership conference for pastors and listening to another speaker. This time the speaker was teaching on finances. Believe it or not, part of the way into his teaching he asked the question, "How many people here know how many one hundred dollar bills there are in circulation for every one dollar bill?"

This got my attention. I knew God was speaking to me, but the question for me was, "Where are they? Where are the one hundred dollar bills, because I surely do not have any!" It was really clear that God was speaking to me. My thinking was being challenged. He wanted me to step out in faith and change my way of thinking.

I was pondering this currency revelation God had shown me and trying to figure out how I could think in terms of hundreds instead of ones. The following is how the Holy Spirit directed me to change my actions. Remember; this is my real life story. It does not get any more practical than this.

A practical plan

I realized that when I went to the bank, I would often withdraw over $100 in cash. I would take out $120 or $150, whatever was needed for the time. I felt the Holy Spirit prompting me to start asking for a one hundred dollar bill from the bank teller, whenever I withdrew over $100 from the bank. If I withdrew over $200, I asked for two one hundred dollar bills. The idea seemed kind of silly and a little bit embarrassing to me. Would God really tell me to do this? But, this impression would not go away. I decided I would obey.

It was hard at first. I felt really self-conscious and embarrassed asking the bank teller for the one hundred dollar bills. "I can do this," I kept telling myself. "God wants me to do this. He is teaching me."

So from time to time, depending on my personal business, I would have a hundred dollar bill or two in my wallet. Eventually, I started to get a little more comfortable with it. This continued for a few months.

He is taking me seriously

One Sunday morning, I was sitting in our local church service with a one hundred dollar bill in my wallet. After the speaker shared his message that morning, it was announced there was going to be a special offering taken for him. I immediately stiffened up because I knew in an instant what God wanted me to do. God was saying, "Okay, Brian, now that you have become accustomed to having a hundred dollar bill in your wallet, I want you to put that one hundred dollar bill in the offering." I admit, it was a struggle. For some reason, it is much harder to depart with a hundred dollar bill than a hundred dollar check. There is something about seeing it go. But I did it. It was an act of obedience, and it felt good.

God spoke to me then and said, "I will take you seriously in this venture if you take Me seriously. I will bless you with hundreds if you are willing to give hundreds." You see, I was thinking in terms of receiving hundreds from God, and He was thinking of me giving hundreds to His work.

I am saying, "Enter at your own risk." This has been so real that I can honestly say without bragging that since that time we have given away the specific amount of one hundred dollars many times. We have been blessed. At the time of this writing, we are giving more money away and receiving more money than we ever have in our lives. By God's grace this principle continues to work in us and through us.

Do something different

I have found that if you desire to enter into something new in your relationship with God, you will have to relate to Him differently than you have in the past. If you desire different results, your actions must be different. Unless your actions change, the results that follow will remain the same. But before your actions can change, your thoughts must change. God was prompting me through this thought-changing process.

The one hundred dollar bill story is one practical example of how the Holy Spirit was teaching me to prosper by changing my thoughts and corresponding actions. The following is another example. The Holy Spirit began to show me that I had a "poverty mindset." The spirit of poverty had warped my thinking to the point that it had a poverty bent to it. My mind had to be changed and have the poverty bent ironed out of it. This next example was part of breaking out of the spirit of poverty and the beliefs that go with it.

The Christmas tree story

One year God blessed us with a magnificent Christmas tree for our home. The tree was on a special sale because the growers were phasing out this particular kind of tree. It was a huge tree, and fortunately we have a cathedral ceiling in our living room or it would not have fit in our home. It looked like a tree that cost eighty to a hundred dollars, but in actuality, it only cost us fourteen dollars—honestly!

The tree was so big we did not have enough of Christmas decorations to cover it. We had to go out and buy more decorations. We decorated the tree and then got ready to enjoy the Christmas season with our family. We were set for a great holiday season.

There was only one problem. I discovered that when people came into our home to visit and saw the towering tree, they always commented about how big it was. However, this wasn't the problem. The problem was my reaction to people's comments.

Their comments often were, "Wow, what a huge Christmas tree." When they said that, the spirit of poverty would rise up inside me and I felt like I had to apologize for God's blessing. I had a compulsion to tell them that I only paid fourteen dollars for the tree or they would think I had paid a lot of money for it. So, out of my mouth would come the words, "Yes, it was on sale and we bought it for only fourteen dollars." I began to hate these words coming out of my mouth. It happened more than once. It was like an automatic response that I could not control. Something in me had to apologize for God's blessing. I did not like my response, and I began to think I needed some type of deliverance or breakthrough.

I could not help but notice the same thing in other areas of my life. If I was wearing a jacket that my wife bought at a secondhand shop for a few dollars and I received a compliment, immediately the response would come out of my mouth that it was used and we bought it for only a few dollars. I could not let people think that God had blessed me with something nice. I began to cry out to God for deliverance. The spirit of poverty says it is more spiritual to be poor or act like you are poor. It was obvious to me, God was teaching me this was not true.

Breaking the spirit of poverty

I started to pray for this spirit of poverty to be broken off of my life. Part of the answer was to realize I had to let people think that I had paid a hundred dollars for the tree. It was extremely difficult for me to do, but finally after someone else commented about our large tree, I was able to bite my lip, swallow the apology and say, "Yes, God blessed us with a more-than-enough tree. God loves me and a big Christmas tree was an expression of His love for our family." Feeling freedom come over me, I knew I was making progress. The Holy Spirit was changing my beliefs, renewing my thoughts, and changing my actions all the while He was teaching me to prosper.

This does not mean we purchased a huge Christmas tree every year after this. Some years we did and some years we did not, but God used this experience to teach me to not apologize for His blessing me. God was changing me in answer to my "teach-me-to-prosper" prayer.

It changed how I buy tires

My tutoring from the Holy Spirit continued. I was having a conversation with a gentleman I met, and we started to talk about cars. He commented about a certain vehicle that he had owned and what a good car it was. He said he had bought it new and owned it until it had 120,000 miles on it. This was a new concept to me since I had never purchased a new car, but his next comment really got my attention. He said he had gone through two sets of tires in the life of the vehicle. I thought he was joking. "What do you mean two sets of tires?" I asked. He replied it had a good set of tires when he bought it from new that lasted for 60,000 miles and then he bought an expensive set of tires that lasted for the second 60,000 miles.

I was amazed. I started to think about what happened when I went to buy tires. I would walk into the tire store and scan the racks of tires until I found the least expensive ones, purchase them and leave thinking about what a bother it was to spend money and time buying tires. Unfortunately the reality was that the cheap tires would soon wear out and before I knew it, I was back in the tire store scanning the racks for the cheapest tires once again. I didn't realize it at the time, but the spirit of poverty was affecting the way I bought tires. I was just thinking about saving a few dollars in the short term and not thinking about the long-term effect. We owned two vehicles, and between the two of them, I was spending too much time and energy at the tire store.

A better quality of life

I contrasted my experience with this man's experience. Somehow, what he was describing seemed like a better path to take. It seemed like a more prosperous path. I changed my method of tire purchasing and started to buy better tires that lasted longer. I spent a lot less of my time and energy shopping for tires. I was able to put more of my emotional energy into things that really mattered like the kingdom of God and my family. The more expensive tires gave my cars a smoother ride and my family felt safer in bad weather. My new tire-buying strategies gave me a better quality of life. I had found a better way, a more prosperous way.

There might be times when it is appropriate to buy inexpensive tires for a vehicle; however, in my personal life, this was one area where the Lord was specifically working to uproot a spirit of poverty in my life.

The wealthy

The final example stems from a book that I believe God directed me to read. The title of the book is *The Millionaire Next Door.* This book basically studied the wealthy in America and examined their lifestyles. Its research showed that most of the wealthy were married with kids, did not inherit their money, still worked 50 hours per week, lived below their means, wore inexpensive suits, gained wealth by saving and investing 20% of their income, worked most of their lives to become wealthy and did not drive exotic foreign cars. In fact, the book revealed that most of the people who drive exotic foreign cars are not wealthy at all. In essence, most of the wealthy look and act like our neighbor next door. [1]

The statistics from the book helped me because in my mind I had this fixation that to be wealthy meant you had to be showy and famous like the movie stars and athletes featured on television. I observed these "life-styles of the rich and famous" folks to have a multitude of family and legal problems as well as being morally bankrupt. I changed my wrong perception of what it "looked like" to be wealthy. God has a better way. The Bible teaches something different about God's blessing. Proverbs states the following,

> The blessing of the Lord brings wealth, and he adds no trouble to it (Proverbs 10:22).

Ah! There is a better way. Somehow this seemed like a path that a good and loving God would provide for His children. The Holy Spirit was teaching me to prosper.

NOTES

[1] *Millionaire Next Door*, Thomas J. Stanley, Ph.D., William D. Danko, Ph.D., (Atlanta, Georgia: Longstreet Press, 1996).

Small Group Study Questions

1. Are you ready to have your beliefs and your thoughts challenged in the area of finances? Please pray about this and don't answer too quickly.

2. Are there any specific beliefs God has already put on your heart to begin to change? What are they?

3. Have you ever felt guilty or wanted to apologize for God's blessings in your life? What are the roots of this type of thinking?

4. How does quality of life fit in with biblical prosperity?

5. How is God's prosperity different from what we see pictured on television and in magazines?

6. Can you identify with any of the poverty mindset examples given in this chapter? Which ones?

CHAPTER 10

Go For It...Start Now!

I guess by now you realize what challenge I am going to give to you. Would you be willing to pray the same risky prayer that I did, "Holy Spirit, teach me to prosper?" Will you take *El Shaddai* at His Word as we have studied it?

Maybe you still have some lingering doubts. Where is the balance in all of this? Is there a side of this biblical truth that we are not seeing? I dare say there is a balance, and I intend to address it. However, it might not be what you expect.

The balance to prosperity is not poverty. Biblically, there is no such thing as a little bit of prosperity and a little bit of poverty to balance it out. My son plays on a soccer team. I encourage him to play his best, stay humble and be successful. I don't tell him to "do well, but not too well." I don't tell him to "score goals, but not too many goals." I cheer him on to be successful on the soccer field.

Giving is the balance

The balance to prosperity is "giving." We should not live to get, we should live to give. In the Old Testament, the ark represented the presence of God. Wherever the ark went, God brought financial blessing. His presence brought blessing. It was part of His nature then and it is part of His nature now. He has not changed, He wants to bless us so we can be a blessing to others.

We need natural riches

The spirit of poverty is a specific and strategic stronghold opposing the church to hold it back and keep it from growing. The devil is not as concerned about the church having spiritual riches as long as he can hinder the church from receiving the natural riches needed to export the spiritual riches. The spirit of poverty must be rooted out of the church so that natural riches can be provided for us to complete our task of fulfilling the Great Commission.

We have to move away from a dualistic mindset that says spiritual riches are good and natural riches are bad. Money is more than merely a necessary evil, it is a vital tool God wants to put in our hands so we can succeed in what we are called to do.

If there is a prophetic re-releasing of the biblical prosperity message to the church community as I suggested earlier, we would find it beginning to emerge various places in the body of Christ.

Listen to what C. Peter Wagner says in his book *Churchquake*. This quote comes from a chapter entitled "Money, No Problem."

> My first 35 years of ordained ministry were spent in the environment of churches that seemed to have chronic money problems. Out of that grew an assumption that no church has enough money to do what it believes it really ought to be doing. During the past few years, however, I have discovered that there are, in fact, many churches that have relatively few money problems and that seem to be able to do just about everything they want to do.[1]

I believe it is a new day for the church in the area of finances. In his book *Profit for the Lord*, William Danker chronicled the story of the Moravians and how they started many kinds of businesses to make money, both at home base and on the mission field, to fund their endeavors. He closes the book with these thoughts:

Once again we may have to look to a small, dedicated group of people like the Moravians, people who will perform heroically in the world mission out of all proportion to their numbers. These charismatic, Spirit-filled individuals will seek every possible channel through which they can make or support their witness.[2]

Will you be one of these dedicated people who will answer the Lord's call to fund the Great Commission?

Prosperity of the soul

I want to caution you not to think about getting a second or third job and working twice as hard to become prosperous. If this is what you are thinking, you are missing the point. Maybe if you had five jobs, then you would have more money. You just wouldn't sleep. No, this is not God's will. This is poverty thinking. I like to think of the example of a farmer with his crops growing while he sleeps at night. He works hard during the day, but his seed is growing in the nighttime while he is sleeping.

I love the scripture found in Ecclesiastes 2:26, "To the man who pleases him, God gives wisdom, knowledge and happiness, but to the sinner he gives the task of gathering and storing up wealth to hand it over to the one who pleases God. This too is meaningless, a chasing after the wind."

Prosperity of soul will cause us to prosper in all areas. It comes out from within us. It is not the result of our striving. What could Joseph have done to promote himself from slavery to the second highest government official in all of Egypt? It would not have happened by his own efforts.

Don't strive to be prosperous

I live in the middle of rich Pennsylvania farmland. There was a farmer in our area who constantly worked his equipment with the throttle wide open. He even drove from the barn to the field as fast as he could. Another wise, prosperous farmer was heard saying this farmer would never be able to make any money because his equipment simply would not last. A few years later, the first farmer had to sell his farm and take another job.

Our bodies were not made to be running at full throttle eighteen hours a day, seven days a week. God has a path of blessing for you to walk in. Let Him do it. Let the Word of God cause faith to rise in your heart to embrace *El Shaddai* and your expectation of God's financial provision of more than enough. Expect Him to teach you to prosper. Allow Him to change your beliefs. If your patterns of thinking change, the words that you speak will begin to change. If your words change, your actions will change. And, if your actions change, the outcome will change.

Listen to how the Living Bible translates Habakkuk 2:3, "Slowly, steadily surely the time approaches when the vision will be fulfilled, do not despair for these things will surely come to pass. Just be patient, they will not be overdue a single day." The Holy Spirit is a patient teacher. There is a proverb that states the path of the righteous is like the dawning sun, shining brighter and brighter until the full day. Let faith for biblical prosperity grow inside of you and nothing will be able to contain it.

Teach me to prosper

Your finances are not the responsibility of the government, your family or the church. If you feel like a victim of fate, the lack of opportunities, the choices of others or circumstances beyond your control, I want to encourage you to take a fresh look at your situation.

Prosperity With a Purpose

It might seem like you are in a hopeless, financial cycle and you cannot do anything to change it. It may feel like this is your lot in life. However, I want to remind you that this type of fatalistic thinking is more Hindu/Buddhist in nature than Christian. You can do something to change your financial condition. Your finances are your responsibility. It is great if others help, but the responsibility is yours. You are the one who must believe in God as *El Shaddai*.

You are currently reaping what you have sown in your finances. Allow the Holy Spirit to show you what changes may be necessary. You have heard my story, and I am sure yours will be different, but just as exciting. Ask the Holy Spirit to teach you to prosper and let the adventure begin.

As I prayed this prayer, it was answered over a number of years, so you might want to pick this book back up again a year from now and see if there are any new insights the Lord would give you.

NOTES
[1] C. Peter Wagner, *Churchquake!* (Ventura, California: Regal Books, 1999), p. 242
[2] *Profit for the Lord,* William J. Danker, (Grand Rapids, Michigan: William B. Eerdmans Publishing Company, out of print), p. 142.

Small Group Study Questions
1. What is the balance to biblical prosperity?

2. How can we unashamedly expect God to provide us with natural riches?

3. How can striving for riches keep us from having a prosperous soul?

4. If the Holy Spirit is a patient teacher, how should we expect Him to teach us to prosper?

5. Will you pray the prayer, "Holy Spirit, teach me to prosper"?

Suggested Reading List

Developing a Prosperous Soul–Volume 1 by Harold Eberle

Developing a Prosperous Soul-Volume 2 by Harold Eberle

Salvation, Health & Prosperity by David Yonggi Cho

Blessing or Curse by Derek Prince

The Millionaire Next Door by Thomas Stanley/William Danko

Rich Dad, Poor Dad by Robert Kiyosaki

Profit for the Lord by William J. Danker

Prosperity in Every Book of the Bible

Genesis 17:1-6
Exodus 36:3-7
Leviticus 26:9,10
Numbers 6:22-27
Deuteronomy 8:18
Joshua 5:11-12
Judges 2:16
Ruth 4:15
1 Samuel 30:17-20
2 Samuel 9:7
1 Kings 17:14-16
2 Kings 4:1-7
1 Chronicles 29:1-5, 12, 28
2 Chronicles 20:24-26
Ezra 1: 5, 6
Nehemiah 9:20-21, 25
Esther 10:3
Job 42:10-16
Psalms 112
Proverbs 3:9,10
Ecclesiastes 5:19
Song of Songs 2:4
Isaiah 61:6,7
Jeremiah 29:11
Lamentations 3:25-26
Ezekiel 47:7-12
Daniel 2:48
Hosea 2:7,8
Joel 2:24-26
Amos 9:13
Obadiah 17
Jonah 4:2
Micah 4:13

Nahum 1:17
Habakkuk 3:19
Zephaniah 3:17-20
Haggai 2:6-9
Zechariah 3:3-4
Malachi 3:8-10
Matthew 6:25-33
Mark 4:26-29
Luke 5:4-7
John 2:8-10
Acts 24:24-26
Romans 4:18-21
1 Corinthians 16:2
2 Corinthians 9:6-11
Galatians 3:13-14
Ephesians 3:20
Philippians 4:19
Colossians 3:23
1 Thessalonians 4:11-12
2 Thessalonians 3:10
1 Timothy 6:17
2 Timothy 1:16
Titus 3:14
Philemon 1:18-19
Hebrews 6:12-15
James 1:17
1 Peter 3:9
2 Peter 1:3
1 John 4:17
2 John 4
3 John 2
Jude 20
Revelation 22:1-3

Lavish life-styles of the rich and famous? No, the portrait of the average millionaire in America shows anything but this...

The Portrait of a Typical Millionaire

1. Is age 57, a male, married with three children.
2. Most were not millionaires until after 50 years of age.
3. 2/3 are self-employed in a business.
4. Most are involved in a normal business like plumbing.
5. Their average annual income is $247,000.
6. Their average net worth is $3.7 million.
7. Their average property value is $320,000.
8. Most are first generation affluent: eighty-one percent did not inherit their wealth.
9. Most live below their means and wear inexpensive suits and drives U.S. made cars.
10. Most have enough money saved to live ten years without working.
11. Most attended public school; however their children attend private school.
12. They still work 45-55 hours per week.
13. They invest about 20 percent of taxable income each year.
14. Most millionaires do not drive luxury cars and most luxury car drivers are not millionaires.
15. Only half of millionaires live in high status neighborhoods.
16. 30% of millionaires have JC Penney's charge cards and 43% have a Sears charge card.

Compiled from *Millionaire Next Door,* Thomas J. Stanley, Ph.D., William D. Danko, Ph.D., (Atlanta, Georgia: Longstreet Press, 1996).

APPENDIX D

Why Does it Matter What I Say About My Finances?

This is a very good and logical question. I will attempt to answer this question in a concise, biblical manner. Let's look at some scriptures that teach about the words we speak and how it applies to all areas of our lives, including our finances.

God puts a lot of importance on what we say. There are many scriptures that mention this. The scripture that we commonly use to lead people to faith in Christ, Romans 10:9, indicates that we should not only believe in our hearts but also confess with our mouths to come into salvation. Even though we believe in our hearts, which is something that happens in the "unseen" world, it seems it is spiritually significant to speak words into the "seen" world in which we live. The words we speak are at the very core of the gospel of Jesus Christ.

In the beginning of the Bible, we find Genesis teaching that God created the world in seven days by His words. He said, "Let there be light," and there literally was light created. As we study these scriptures, it appears like God's very words were the creative force that brought the world as we know it into existence.

Later, God changed Abram's name to Abraham. God started calling Abraham "the father of many" when he was not even the father of a son. He was not the father of anyone! Worse yet, by changing his name, God made Abraham call himself "the father of many" every time he introduced himself to someone or someone asked his name. Can you picture Abraham feeling a little embarrassed as he, a man without a son or daughter, spoke the words, "My name is 'father of many'"? I can picture this! Yet Abraham's faith-filled words eventually bore the fruit of making him the father of many.

Many other Bible characters used this biblical truth when expecting their current situation and circumstances to change. David had the following words to say at his encounter with Goliath:

> David said to the Philistine, "You come against me with sword and spear and javelin, but I come against you in the name of the Lord Almighty, the God of the armies of Israel, whom you have defied. This day the Lord will hand you over to me, and I'll strike you down and cut off your head. Today I will give the carcasses of the Philistine army to the birds of the air and the beasts of the earth, and the whole world will know that there is a God in Israel. All those gathered here will know that it is not by sword or spear that the Lord saves; for the battle is the Lord's, and he will give all of you into our hands" (1 Samuel 17:45-47).

This was not a silent prayer to God. In fact, he did not direct these words to God at all. David said these words to Goliath, his enemy. He was speaking faith-filled words about what God wanted to do. The events he spoke of had not actually happened as yet. However they did come to pass.

What about Jesus cursing the fig tree in the gospel of Mark? He spoke to the fig tree. He didn't pull it up. He didn't ask His disciples to cut it down. No, his words were enough to cause it to die by the time he returned that way.

Jesus continued on after finding the dead fig tree to teach about faith. He underlined again the importance of faith-filled words and how battles are won and victories gained by using them.

> "Have faith in God," Jesus answered. "I tell you the truth, if anyone says to this mountain, 'Go, throw yourself into the sea,' and does not doubt in his heart but believes that

what he says will happen, it will be done for him. Therefore I tell you, whatever you ask for in prayer, believe that
you have received it, and it will be yours" (Mark 11:22-
24).

God's Promise

We are to *say* to the mountain, "throw yourself into the sea."
Mountains are the things that stand in the way of us fulfilling God's will
for our lives.

Remember when Jesus called Simon, "Peter"? He called Peter a
rock when it looked like he was anything but a solid guy that could be
involved in building the kingdom of God. I believe when Jesus said
those words, it actually released the power that helped make Peter
into "the rock" that he would became.

How about this scripture in Romans, chapter 4, that describes
God and how He does things on the earth.

> Therefore, the promise comes by faith, so that it may be
> by grace and may be guaranteed to all Abraham's off-
> spring—not only to those who are of the law but also to
> those who are of the faith of Abraham. He is the father of
> us all. As it is written: "I have made you a father of many
> nations." He is our father in the sight of God, in whom he
> believed—the God who gives life to the dead and calls
> things that are not as though they were (Romans 4:16-
> 17).

This scripture teaches that God calls things "that are not as though
they were." It sounds a lot like what God did in Genesis when He
created the heavens, the earth, light, man, etc. Does this mean that He
wants us to also speak creative, faith-filled words? I believe it does.
Let's look at the following proverbs:

> From the fruit of his mouth a man's stomach is filled;
> with the harvest from his lips he is satisfied. The tongue

has the power of life and death, and those who love it will eat its fruit (Proverbs 18:20-21).

From the fruit of his lips a man is filled with good things as surely as the work of his hands rewards him (Proverbs 12:14).

I have to admit though, in spite of all these scriptures, it still feels awkward to say "My debts are paid off," when I have a payment schedule in my desk drawer for loan payments. And yet, somehow when I say those words, faith rises up in my heart that the mountain of debt can and will be removed from my life. It is a spiritual principle, and it is not always easy to understand how it works. But it does work. I am not denying reality, I am changing it.

2 Corinthians gives us some additional insight into how God's promises come to pass in our lives.

For no matter how many promises God has made, they are "Yes" in Christ. And so through him the "Amen" is spoken by us to the glory of God. Now it is God who makes both us and you stand firm in Christ....

The promises God has given are "yes" in Christ; however, the "amen" is spoken by us. Did you get that? We must *say* the amen. Our words make His promises a reality in our lives.

In summary, it does matter what we say about our finances because the Bible says we will eat the fruit of our words. God speaks and things come to pass, and He wants us to speak forth His will for our lives and life situations and it will come to pass.

Other Books by Brian Sauder

Elders for Today's Church

Healthy leadership teams produce healthy churches!
New Testament principles for equipping church leadership teams: Why leadership is needed, what their
qualifications and responsibilities are, how they should
be chosen, how elders function as spiritual fathers and
mothers, how they are to make decisions, resolve con-
flicts, and more. Included are in-depth questionnaires for
evaluating a team of elders. *by Larry Kreider, Ron Myer, Steve
Prokopchak, and Brian Sauder 288 pages:* $12.99

Helping You Build Cell Churches

A complete biblical blueprint for small group ministry, this manual covers 54 topics! Gives full, in-
tegrated training to build cell churches from the
ground up. *Compiled by Brian Sauder and Larry Kreider, 256 pages.* $19.95

Youth Cells And Youth Ministry

Learn the values behind youth cells and custom-design
cells for your youth. Along with a revealing insight into
today's youth culture, this book gives the specifics of
implementing youth cell ministry, including a cell
leader's job description, creative ideas for cells, ministry
from junior high to young adults, and how churches can
transition. *Compiled by Brian Sauder & Sarah Mohler,
120 pages.* $8.50
Youth Cells and Youth Ministry Audio Set $45.00

House To House Publications   Call 1-800-848-5892
Order online: www.dcfi.org   email: H2HP@dcfi.org

Prosperity With a Purpose